AF492454

Parental Negligence:
A short story on parents careless attitude towards their children.

WILLIAM DAVIDSON

All rights reserved. No part of this publication may be reproduced, distributed, or transmitted in any form or by any means, including photocopying, recording, or other electronic or mechanical methods, without the prior written permission of the publisher, except in the case of brief quotations embodied in critical reviews and certain other noncommercial uses permitted by copyright law.

Copyright © William Davidson,2022.

<u>NOTE TO READERS</u>

This work is surely and purely an educative fiction for its readers,so all the characters are entirely figments of the author's imagination. Any resemblance of actual locations,persons,whether dead or alive are purely accidental.

<u>DEDICATION</u>

By the abundant Grace of God, I dedicate this book to parents passing through difficult phases to console and assure them that no condition is permanent

Table of content

CHAPTER ONE

Ike, have you noticed that today's business is dull? Emmanuel asked his friend and jungle mate Ikenna from their hideout. Ikenna was popularly called Ike by family and friends owing to his physical prowess and muscles in his body makeup. 'Ike' means Power and had been used to explain the person of Ikenna, as being very strong and having never been defeated by an army of his mates over the years.

Ikenna at the age of fifteen had already dropped out of school. Most people blamed his parents for not being able to cater for his secondary education, while others believed it was his unseriousness that made him drop out; but whatever the case had become, the only interference drawn was that Ikenna was always found in the streets with some other boys of his age or caught in one criminal act or the other.

"Today indeed is a very bad day, not even a single coin has been realized since morning.

This is past noon and very soon dusk will come over us. Anyway, my sister always says that a bad day is not known by its morning. Let us be hopeful." Ike replied Emmanuel, pulling these trousers which were always loose at the waistline. People thought it was always like that because he had lost some weight, but what also confused them was why he would always pull it up to the waist at every step he made.

Ike was so fond of his sister, Vivian. He always talked about her whenever he was with his friends and sometimes, his friends would challenge him or make jest of him for always talking about Vivian his sister. Vivian was always on his lips consciously and unconsciously. That afternoon, he had raised the issue of Vivian before his friend Emmanuel.

"There you go again, Ike? It's always about your sister. You know you have your way of bringing in Vivian your sister into every discussion." Emmanuel teased his friend, Ike. Ike chuckled at Emmanuel's statement.

"Emmanuel you amaze me most time. You of all people should not be oblivious of the fact that Vivian is my one and only sister. You also know she is the only reason I work hard to ensure she doesn't drop out of school as I did. Mother and father might have failed us, but I will make sure that life doesn't fail my sister no matter what it takes."

Vivian was the only sister of Ike and the second child of Maria and John. Oftentimes, it had been wondered why such a lovely being in the person of Vivian should come into a family like that of John which had little or no reputation.

The breadfruit has never fallen for those who possess the processing technique. People would always say, shudder and go their ways.

Vivian was just the exact opposite of her brother Ike, who was a well-known truant, a deviant in society. Unlike Ike, she was very quiet, intelligent, and obedient. These were

the reasons people loved and cherished her
a lot.

Two middle-aged women were coming back
from the market one day when Vivian
walked past them and greeted them
genuflecting.

"Good afternoon Mama Ada, Good
afternoon Mama David."

"My dear, thank you." Mama Ada replied.

"My dear welcome," Mama David replied.
She walked past.

"Whenever I see this girl, I often wonder
why God has not blessed me with a girl
child. Vivian is one child in this
neighborhood that throws a stone of
jealousy at me. The way she greets and
respects everyone is very rare among her
peers." Mama David commented.

"What about me that have four girls? One,
two, three, four... Tell me, which one of
them behaves like Vivian? Ada may seem to
be less troublesome than others, but it
doesn't make her as respectful as Vivian.
This is why I always urge them to identify

with Vivian and not some bunch of these uncultured kids that are bred these days." Mama Ada said.

"You see, we are both saying almost the same thing. You have a role model in Vivian for your girls. Who will she model for me? The boys? Now you understand my plight of wait..." She laughed and made some funny gestures.

"Should I rather make her brother, Ike the model for my son? God forbid!" Both women burst into laughter such that passerby looked at them.

"But let me ask, what exactly is wrong with that boy? He is always here and there stealing one thing or the other, pickpocketing and fighting his fellows every now and then. I hate to admit he is a brother to the all admired Vivian, two opposite coins" Mama Ada shook her head in disappointment.

"The boy is just a bad omen. Just last week, I saved him from Jack. You know Jack that owns provision shop at the village square?"

Mama Ada nodded in acknowledgment of whom she was talking about and so she continued. "Jack said he attempted to make away with some of his biscuits while he was attending to some other customers, but was lucky that one of his customers saw him and he was caught red-handed. I was the God-sent for Ike that day, if not, Jack was ready to beat the living daylight out of Ike. But do you know the 'thank you' I got from Ike?" She asked looking at Mama Ada in anticipation of her 'continue' facial expression.

"Dear, what was it?" Mama Ada asked listening attentively. "He gave David the beating of his life. I could barely recognize my son when I saw him crying at home yesterday. I didn't believe it when David told me it was Ike that beat him up. Ike that I helped last week laid his hands on my son. And do you know what angered me the most?" Mama David asked ready to narrate further.

"Please, tell me..." Mama Ada picked more interest in their discussion.

"I went to confront Ike and he opened his dirty mouth to tell me that David did not greet him when he walked past him." Mama David spat on the ground in disbelief of her experience. Mama Ada couldn't believe her ears.

"Mama David, I don't want to be mistaken here. Which Ike are we talking about here? Is it Ike, the only son of John who has never said, 'Good Morning' to me, or is it another Ike that I do not know? Ike is just a few months older than David, your son. God! Children nowadays are insane. Does Ikenna greet the aged let alone his peers? We are living in a perilous time. What did you do to him? I hope you skinned him alive. I hope you made sure that every single life inside of him was snuffed out and that he lost..." Mama Ada was still on her words when Mama David tapped her shoulder to behold John as he staggered towards them from afar. Obviously, John had drunk himself to stupor that hot afternoon. John, over the years, had become an object of shame to his family and mockery by the town. Little wonder he had already taken enough alcohol to make him stagger just a few seconds past noon.

"That's it! Talk of the devil... This man is not just a bunch of lazy human beings but also shameless. Can you see why most times I don't blame Ike, the poor boy is from a very bad home and has no model to show him a better living. Take a look at his father, is this one a perfect match for a father figure? God forbid...! Mama David lamented.

"This is just very bad. How can a full-fledged family man with such responsibility be jobless and at the same time a drunk? He spends every minute of his day in the bar seeking who would buy drinks for him and he wouldn't make to leave there until he had taken enough liquor to make him stagger. Oh... see how a woman of my kind has been married to this kind of man? She must be heartbroken to see the father of her children

stagger in a broad daylight in this manner…"
Said, Mama Ada.

"Which woman? Don't tell me you are on Maria's side. Listen, Mama Ada, let me ask you, what degree of drunkness will your husband get into that would compel you to be wayward?"

"God forbid!" Mama Ada snapped her fingers in a bid to reject a bad omen. Mama David continued…

"Am surprised you are the only woman in this neighborhood that is not aware that Maria does not care about her family's welfare. She now carries herself with so much ego with all the makeup in the world on her face. She no longer has time for her family at all. Don't you see how her son is always on the streets, fending for himself and his sister while her husband is always in the drinking parlor? Poor children!"

"Chai!" These children are suffering. I still insist that John is the cause of all this. I mean, if this man takes up the responsibility required of him, there won't be any point or need for the woman to go out looking for the money by every possible means or the son going into the streets to fend for himself and his sister. Imagine if he was able to keep Ike in school… Imagine if he brings food to the table every day. Who knows? Very soon, Vivian will no longer go to school. That will be very bad." Mama Ada said as she shook her head in pity.

Well, that's your point of view. For as long as we know, everyone is entitled to his own opinion. As for me, I believe God has the strength to make them overcome times like this only if they will call upon Him. Even if John has erred, it is now up to Maria to pick up the remnants of the family, put them together, and get it working. But what has she done? Help John in the family destruction mission. Well, I also think it's too late for her to rethink her actions. She is careless!' Mama David asserted.

By this time, Mama David has already gotten to the T-junction that led to her house and so, the two women parted ways, pondering on the things which they had talked about.

MORAL LESSON

1. It is the responsibility of every man to take charge of this home

2.We should not involve ourselves in social vices(crimes) because we want to earn a living.

3. We should learn to be responsible.

4. A wise woman builds her home.

5. We should be role models people should look up to for good behaviors

QUESTIONS

1.Who was Ikenna?

___

2.What did Ikenna do with his friend Emmanuel?

___

3.Why did many people admire and cherish Vivian?

___

4.Who were the women that talked much about Vivian and her family members?

___

5.What will you say about Maria, Ikenna and Vivian's Mother?

____

CHAPTER TWO

"I will not for anything cease to regret the very day you stepped your two legs into my father's house asking for my hand in marriage! Oh, how foolish I was not to look beyond the light skin and the well-shaved beards of yours. Only if I did, I would have seen misery, frustration, and pain packaged in human form. Tell me, how a man who is supposed to be a father of two, cannot be able to cater for the family.
Today you are sober, tomorrow you are drunk to a stupor, and you know I have never stopped wondering where you get the money to spend on alcohol from. You know this is sheer wickedness. You cannot afford to feed your family, but you do have money to consume alcohol and you say you do not know what you do? Of course, you do. You are just being wicked." Maria could be heard from all corners of the neighborhood as she

rained abuse on her husband. The children were seated at a corner of the compound as they watched their parents exchange words for words, while passersby always stole some look at the seeming free show.
John chuckled almost inside himself, and said to his wife, "They say that death that is about dealing with a puppy will never allow it to smell the stench that comes from feces, lest he does not eat it. What else does a woman like you have to offer if not a running mouth and running womanhood? Shame on you, I wonder what gives you the guts to call me names
It is not just me this time around, but the whole village knows you are an ill-luck to both yourself and your children. And I still don't understand what has blinded your eyes that you can't see yourself as such. Oh, wait! You are really of the thought that I would ask you out of this house because you are neglecting your duty as a mother No, no, no, not yet! With your eyes, you will behold what you have done to yourself and with the

same eyes, you will bring forth tears to them.

Come to think of it, everyone knows I have no job, but I still find a way to pay for my drinks. But how about you? What have you achieved as a mother? Neither do you pay your children's school fees nor even clothe them. All you do is wake up in the morning leave the house and return when you like. I do not have time, not any for you. Of course, you understand the laws of karma, play with it, it will surely come looking for you tomorrow!"

At this point, the children couldn't take it anymore, they were both seen bursting into tears. The kind of things they heard their parents say made them feel bad. It was more surprising to see Ike, who was always poised powerful, and strong headed cry out some tears. Passerby shook their heads in pity. Vivian somehow and from nowhere mustered up the courage to say something. "Mother, father..." she called as she at the same time sobbed.

"Are you both not tired of behaving shamefully? Your attitudes bring shame to us and our entire family. Am tired of this whole thing. I mean..." Vivian was saying when their mother cut in.

"It's your father that is bringing shame to you and the entire family, not me your mother."

"Mother you are one of the contributors to the problems we experience in this house... I think it is... A fight between you and father. Still, none of you could put food on our table. Is it not time you reconcile your differences and take up your roles as husband and wife, then take care of..."

Maria cut her daughter short in anger, "Will you shut that mouth of yours? Oh! Vivian, has it finally gotten to the extent of insulting me? You now open your mouth to call me names in my very own presence? To tell me that I am not responsible eh! You no longer..."

"No mother, I was only saying that..." Vivian tried to defend herself.

"You ingrate! Who are you to tell me what to
do and how to do it? Look at this small brat!
You are just about twelve and already you
have started giving me words of advice and
talking back at me. By the time you become
twenty, you might be throwing fists of punch
at my face with every confidence. Can't you
imagine?" Maria clapped her hands in
Surprise and somewhat disbelief.
John her husband cut in, "Imagine what?
Tell me, what is it you want to imagine that
has not been happening? Is she not your
breed? Why are you surprised? This is just
you in another form. Your children have
learned nothing from you, but how can I
blame them? They can't be empty-headed,
they just have to learn a thing or two from
their mother and yes, this is it! Oh, you
think it is an unwise adage when our fathers
said that one cannot give what he does not
have. You want her to speak wisdom,
perhaps, in a respectful way. From where if I
may ask? When the womb that nurtured her

does only foolish things? Try to fill yourself before seeking for whom to fill."
Maria became very annoyed at the words of her husband.
I thought you were sober somehow today, but I had mistaken your quietness for sober reflection. Just listen to yourself. Oh, Vivian is now my daughter and my breed and has no wisdom because I have filled her with foolishness. Alright, if that is the case, what have you fed your son, Ike with?
Hahaha! Theft, pilfering, fighting, and stubbornness? Is it not? Excuse me!
Imagine pot calling kettle black, knowing how badly the charcoal has dealt with you a lot? I am very sure Ike has started smoking and drinking like his father and his father sits here to point accusing fingers at his mother, laying claims and blaming unnecessarily. You amaze me, we are not a match and can never be.
Before Maria could finish the words in her mouth, John rushed to where she was and forcefully landed on her cheeks, two

resounding slaps successively that pushed Maria to the ground. She wailed and cried, raining abuses on her husband "foolish man, a good-for-nothing! Beat me if that is all you want, you may even decide to kill me, it doesn't change the fact that you are less than a man." She continued crying and cursing her husband.

Her words irritated her husband the more and with a greater force, he pounced on his wife and gave her the beating of her life. Maria who was already dressed to leave for the day's business was seen rolling on the muddy ground. This had become an everyday affair and so it was not surprising when Ike pulled up his sister and they walked away from the ugly scene.

Vivian wanted to intervene, but she had not forgotten what happened the last time she tried that, her father under the influence of alcohol beat her until she fainted. Surprisingly, her mother picked up her bag and ran away leaving her at the mercy of John, her father.

With these memories in her head, it would
be unwise for her to move even an inch close
to the spot where her mother cried.
Just with the speed of light, Ike and Vivian
left the compound.

MORAL LESSONS

1. It is wrong for husband and wife to trade words before their children.

2. Children should not talk to their parents in a disrespectful manner irrespective of their parents ill-behavior

3. Husbands should not beat their wives.

4. Parents bad behaviors will definitely influence their children.

5. We should apply caution in whatever we do in life.

QUESTIONS

1. From Maria's statement in the first paragraph of this chapter, was she really enjoying her marriage?

____

____

2. From her statement, how will you describe her husband John?

____

____

3. What proverb did John say to his wife?

____

____

4. According to Vivian, who was one of the contributors of the problems they experience in the house?

____

____

5. According to Maria, what did John feed his son Ike with?

____

____

6. Who beat Maria?

____

____

CHAPTER THREE

Community Primary School, Abana was a very popular school in Abana and its environs. This was particularly because the school was an aged long school in Abana. Most parents had told their children that they were the first set of pupils who attended the school.

Some major challenges of the school were poor infrastructure, lack of a well-equipped library, understaffing, and lack of study aids and materials. The School even though was a property of the state government received not much care or provision from the government. The pupil's desks were all faulty and many of them were broken and dumped. The school building was dilapidated and most necessary teaching materials were not available.

These made the teaching profession being exercised in the school very tedious for the few teachers who were still available. Also, the school which was meant to be tuition subsidized compulsorily levied on the parents of kids who attended the school to meet up with the requirement of the Education Board of the State

Over the last five to six years, the school had received some threats to be closed down, as a result of its inability to attain the standard school requirement of the State Education Board. This however will be a major slap in the face of Abana Town.

Community Primary school Abana had just a few teachers who were retained by the school. Stories had it that they were owed salaries, even though they were being paid little. In other news, it was said that the attitude of the government towards the teachers embittered them that they tend to pour their anger on their pupils.

"That was how Aunty Igwe, that is, Douglas's Wife flogged my daughter until she fainted, sometime last year. I wondered what offense Susan had committed when I got the news in the market and was dumbfounded to learn from the teacher that she was pounced on my daughter because she couldn't answer her question. I thought I had heard it all until I also learned the question she asked my daughter do you know what it was? "Who was the second vice-president of Uganda? Can you just imagine? How can she expect a girl in just primary two to answer that question correctly? She claimed she had taught them on that but it still did not make any sense to me. I sincerely wanted to withdraw Susan from that school, but my purse was saying otherwise. I simply don't understand why these teachers have to lash out their bitterness on these poor children, especially now that we pay double what we used to pay. They are just never satisfied." A few people listened with rapt attention as Mama Susan shared her story.

This was the same school Vivian and Ike attended. Vivian continued going to school even after Ike dropped out of school. Ike was not a very bright pupil but would have been courageous enough to continue if he had been properly taken care of. Nobody cares for their school fees let alone the material they used in school. Maria, their mother would always push them to their father whenever they came asking for money, claiming that school and everything that has to do with it was the sole responsibility of their father, while their father on the other hand always said he had no money.

Ike, therefore, was compelled to leave school to support his dear sister. He would pick people's pockets, steal from people's shops and bully little children who were sent on errands, then collect their money. This he had done for some time now which had landed him in so many cases, especially with Mr.Jack, the provision shop seller.

Vivian was always heartbroken to see her brother stealing people's things and then getting himself into trouble just for her sake. Most times, she would confront her brother who would always claim he did some menial jobs to raise the money. Even though Vivian knew he was lying there was nothing she could do about it.

On a fateful Monday morning, Mrs. Vanessa who was Vivian's teacher called out names of pupils who had not paid their school fees and their Common Entrance Examination fees.

For Vivian, primary six was her most difficult session during all her school time. She found it very difficult because of the various fees she was mandated to pay. She had not paid the school's Common Entrance Examination fee, Mock Examination fee, PTA levy, Sports House levy and so many others. Thanks to Ike who had cleared the minor fees for her, remaining the school fees and the Common Entrance Examination fees which were the major fees in the session.

"Vivian, I have just told you not to worry much. Just tell your class teacher to give us more time. Probably, by next week, we should be able to come up with something."

Ike pacified Vivian that Monday morning
before she left for school.

"Ike, I don't like the idea of you stealing and
selling people's fowl or picking people's
pockets. You know how much of our image
this your act has tarnished." Vivian said with
bitterness in her heart despite that part of
Ikenna's loot went to her education.

"Eeem, you don't have to worry, but you
should not forget that I do everything for
your sake. You can't afford to leave school
now, not now we have struggled up to this
point. You are now in Primary six and in a
few months, you will be out of that place.
But just in case you should know, nobody is
stealing anybody's fowl this time around.
My friend Emmanuel told me of a field, that
is overgrown with grasses and the owner
needs laborers who would cut the grasses, as
he wants to start working on the field. I
hope to go there by tomorrow with
Emmanuel to clear the field and after that, I
will be paid, Ike lied to his sister who
happily left for school

"Vivian John!" Mrs. Vanessa repeated after
Vivian didn't answer loudly to her first call.
"Present Aunty!" Vivian answered louder
this time around as she stepped out from
her desk. There were just three of the pupils
who were still owing the school as at then.
"Now the three of you, line up here!" Mrs.
Vanessa commanded as she made for her
cane from the table.
"Please ma, please ma... I will pay
tomorrow." The three pupils cried, almost
simultaneously. She started with Vivian who
was already full of tears even before the cane
landed on her.
"Ma please, my brother said that he will give
me the money by next week. I will pay ma."
Vivian cried pleading.
"By next week you said? Are you listening to
yourself? Your Common Entrance
Examination comes up in three weeks and
up till now, you are yet to register and you
tell me not to flog out the devil that wants to
deal with your future out from you? And did
I just hear you say your brother will give you

the money? So, it is you that pushes your brother into stealing from people in order to pay your fees? That useless brother of yours that has no ambition for himself. If I may ask, who does he want to rob this time around?" Mrs. Vanessa tongue-lashed Vivian while the whole class burst into hilarious laughter. They mocked Vivian which brought about her shedding more hot tears from her already reddish eyes to her plump cheeks.

"Ma, he got a menial job at a field to work on. He wants to cut the whole grasses with his friends and he has been promised to be paid very well." Vivian replied in a shaky voice and her cries won't allow her to speak properly.

"Lair! Vivian, you lied! Vivian, I have known you to be a very good girl, why lie to defend that brother of yours who has no sense of morality?" Mrs. Vanessa fired at her.

"Ma it's true. He will give me the money next week." Vivian cried out the more.

"Will you turn your back for me! And listen attentively, I am giving the three of you six strokes of cane as yet another message of warning, after which you pick up your bags and go home. I do not want to see any of you here until you have paid every dime you owe this school. Your mind tells you we run a charity home here. Do you know how much we spend to give you what you receive here? And when you are told to pay just a token for appreciating what we do, you will find it difficult to comply. Not today, I will let my whip fo the talking. Quickly, turn your back! Mrs. Vanessa gave them each, hot six strokes of the cane that sent Vivian into the air, jumping and screaming calling upon the names of her ancestors to come to her aid.

The three pupils, including Vivian, picked up their school bags and cried all the way home.

MORAL LESSONS

1. We should not do evil to earn a living.

2. Parents should work hard in order to pay their children school fees and levies.

3. Schools sometimes should be considerate while treating matters that have to do with financing the children's education.

4. Pupils should take time to explain the situation of things affecting their studies/education to their teachers.

5. We should not laugh at our fellow pupils.

6. Teacher should be careful the way they discipline a pupil.

QUESTIONS

1. What was the name of the school Vivian attended?

____

____

2. What were the challenges of the school?

____

____

3. What threats did the school receive over the past five to six years?

____

____

4. What lie did Ikenna tell Vivian his sister?

____

5. Why did Mrs Vanessa flog Vivian and two other pupils?

____

____

CHAPTER FOUR

Vivian returned home early enough and met Ike in the house. Maria and John, their parents had already left the house. That was the usual. Ike sighted his sister from the gate and rushed to meet her.

"Vivian! What happened to you? Who beat you? Why are you crying?" Ike hurriedly asked his sister who intensified the tempo of her sobbing. It was as though more pains were poured on her as she cried out the more, throwing herself to the ground. This pierced Ike's heart.

"Vivian, talk to me. Stop keeping silent. Just mention the person's name. Who beat you? Is it that village bully, Kelvin? Did he stop you on your way to school? Vivian talk now... or wait! Did anybody fight you in school?" Ike pressed the more.

"Mrs. Vanessa ... Mrs. Vanessa flogged me
with a big whip because of that money!"
Vivian said. Ike was very angry.
"Which money? The money I told you to
promise her you would pay by next week?
Why is this woman this wicked? I do not
blame her at all, she sits in the classroom
day-to-day and at the end of the month, she
is paid some money. For that reason, she
does not know or understand how difficult it
is for people to eat, let alone pay that big
money in school. Don't worry, she must pay
for this!" Ike thundered with tears forming
in his eyes. He tried to help his sister stand
up from the floor where she had thrown
herself when Vivian gave out a loud scream.
"Ahrr..."
"What is it?" Ike asked her.
"You touched my back where Mrs. Vanessa
flogged me." She said.
"She flogged you at your back? Vivian, let
me see!" He demanded.
Vivian, who unbuttoned her uniform,
showed him the zebra marks which were

scattered all over her back. Ike grew more in anger but tried to hide it from Vivian.

"Come inside let me use hot water to massage and apply some balm on it." Vivian stood up from the ground, made to move, halted, and then turned to Ike.

"Ike what are you thinking? What are you planning? Ike, I already have enough problems, please don't land me into more trouble. Ike please..." Vivian asked inquisitively.

"Vivian, I have always listened to you and never failed to. But you see this time around, just let me be. I want to think. That woman is evil and she needs to be visited with evil. Come inside! Ike answered.

"But Ike..." Vivian tried to intervene.

"Vivian stop! Don't infuriate me the more. I am already boiling." Ike retorted.

At this point, Vivian knew Ike had made up his mind to deal with Mrs. Vanessa and there was nothing anybody could do to stop him.

It was a few minutes past the hour of two when Mrs. Vanessa, Vivian's class teacher was coming back from school through her usual narrow path which led to her husband's house. Mrs. Vanessa preferred taking this route home. Even though it was always lonely and most times, scary, it was the shortest route to her place. If she decided to take the village square, it would double her journey, if not more than, the time she would spend when she took the narrow path.

Mrs. Vanessa hummed a song as she walked. She had with her a blue translucent file which contained the assignments of her pupils which were submitted that day, in one hand and the other hand was a black handbag which contained her purse, a mobile phone, a bunch of keys and a white handkerchief. Inside the purse, she had the money given to her by the two pupils who were flogged with Vivian and some other money that her husband had given her to cook if she returned from school. Her

mobile phone was newly purchased by her
brother, after many years of being without a
phone. Her husband ignored her because
she lost her previous phone just one month
after her husband bought it for her. And so,
it was after all these months that her brother
finally came to her rescue and bought a new
phone, bigger, better, more sophisticated
and of course more expensive than the
previous one she had lost.
These things she walked with majestically,
all of a sudden, stones began to land on her
body from different directions. The very first
heavy one landed on her right shoulder
which brought her to a halt. She looked up
in the direction from where the stones had
landed and before she could see anything,
another heavy one landed on her back which
made her turn abruptly to the opposite
direction with the first one, from where it
had come and then just immediately, came
the third one which landed on her head and
sent her on her knees.

Just before she could do or say anything, turns and turns of stones landed on her body which finally brought her to the ground with her head buried in her elbows as she cried unto her ancestors.

Ike and his friend, Emmanuel never stopped firing the stones until they made sure the woman found no strength to cry anymore. With their faces masked with black nylon, they jumped down from a mango tree, moved to the woman, collected her black handbag, her wristwatch, and other pieces of jewelry she had on her, and finally her shiny shoes and vanished into the bush.

Mrs. Vanessa cried and cried in pain until she found little strength to continue her journey home since she was almost close to her place.

The next day, the news went viral in the town that Mrs. Vanessa was attacked by some masked boys who were unidentified. When Vivian heard it, she needed not a second thought to know who the culprits were, she rushed home from the village square where she had gone to pick something.

"Ike, what have you done? That's so cruel, you know?" She said to Ike.

"Vivian, what did I do to you?" Ike pretended to be oblivious of whatever it was Vivian spoke about.

"You know what I am saying, Ike. It was you and your friend that attacked Mrs. Vanessa. I can bet that with my life!" Vivian spilled it, expecting Ike to react to that. Ike simply picked up his footwear and made to leave.

"Vivian, don't be too sure, especially when you have no proof. But come to think of it, stones for whips are somehow commensurate, don't you think so?" Ike barged out of the house.

Vivian broke down and started crying. She felt she was between the devil and the deep blue sea. She didn't doubt the fact that Ike was cruel to her teacher, but was not unaware of the fact that it was her brother standing up to the teacher's cruelty to herself, Vivian.

MORAL LESSONS

1. On no account should school children plan evil for their teachers or attack them verbally or physically.

2. Dialogue is the best solution in solving problems not a fight.

3. Stealing other people's belongings is evil.

4. We should listen to the voice of wisdom like that of Vivian to her brother Ike.

5. Revenge is of the Lord.

QUESTIONS

1. Who returned home early?

____

____

2. Who wanted to know what happened to her?

____

____

3. Who attacked Mrs Vanessa on her way home?

____

____

4. What were the items Mrs Vanessa had in her black handbag?

5. "Ike, what have you done? That's so cruel, you know?" Who asked the above question and why?

CHAPTER FIVE

Ike and Emmanuel his friend were successful in disposing of the things they robbed of Mrs. Vanessa by the means of selling them. They knew they would easily be implicated if they attempted to display them in the village market or take it to anyone from the village to buy. They were wise enough to go to the next neighboring town market where they confidently displayed them and sold them out at cheap prices. The money they made from the item, including the new phone, they merged with the money they found inside the woman's bag and it amounted to quite a reasonable sum. Ike and Emmanuel shared the proceeds from their loots equally.

When Ike returned home that day, he brought all the remaining fees for his sister from the money and still had enough. He called her.

"Vivian, take this money. You will go back to
school on Monday, that is if your teacher
has recovered, I heard she was
hospitalized." Vivian was so happy as she
received the money.
"Thank you, Ike. But how did you get all this
money? The field you worked on, is it that
big to fetch you such a huge amount?"
Vivian questioned.
"Let's just say that God knows the best way
to take care of us." Ike needed not to say
more than that, lest Vivian continued
questioning him.
"I saw my classmates when they were
coming back from school today and they
told me they heard that Mrs. Vanessa is not
likely to come back this term because she is
in a critical condition. They said Aunty
Precious of primary five has been the one
teaching them since this week and it is
rumored she would combine her class with
ours, so she can effectively handle the both
of us." Vivian informed Ike.

"Really? That sounds like good news. By the time she is back to her feet, you are done with your Common Entrance Examination and out of that school." Ike replied.

"Is that it? If that sounds like good news, let me also share with you one that sounds like bad news. My classmates also said that every finger points at you. They said Mrs. Vanessa believes that no one else would do that in this town if not you, though she didn't see the culprits' faces. They are also aware of how much you care for me and they assumed that was your way of fighting for your sister." Vivian informed Ike the more, but surprisingly, Ike burst into heavy laughter.

"What is funny about what I told you?" Queried Vivian.

"Vivian see, just like I told you the other day, everyone can assume and suspect for all I care, but no one has any proof. Not even you Vivian." Ike boasted.

Vivian finally gave up. She was happy she was going back to school as a whole and that finally she was going to write her forthcoming examination with her classmates and her brother was safe. What greater joy would a girl of twelve seek?

MORAL LESSONS

1. We should not rejoice over any evil we commit.

2. We should not sell or buy stolen items.

3. In critical cases, we should apply wisdom.

4. Don't pay evil with evil.

5. Evil or bad news always breaks people's heart.

QUESTIONS

1. Who and who were considered 'successful' in disposing stolen items?

____

____

2. Where did they go to sell the stolen items?

____

____

3. What did Ikem use part of the money he made from the stolen items to do?

____

____

4. What sounded like a good news according to Ike?

____

____

5. What was the opinion of Mrs Vanessa?

____

____

CHAPTER SIX

Every day they say is for the thief, but one day is for the owner. This old-aged adage had over the years proven to be true. Amaeke was a very big town, bigger than Abana. It was only in Amaeke that one could find facilities such as gas stations, banks, civic centers as well as good schools. As a result of these developments, the government was always at their beck and call in making available social amenities they needed. Amaeke even though was a stone's throw from Abana, just after Udeke was far more developed than Abana. One would be surprised at such differences. People left Abana, through Udeke to Amaeke to build shops and make very big investments in the land. It was often asserted by the people of Abana that if the kind of investments the natives of Abana established in Amaeke were brought to Abana, Abana will not be recognized in a short while.

However, those investors understood that such a result will be obtained in a long term, who was willing to wait for long? It was here Emmanuel and I had come to sell the stolen items.

"Ike, did you see that new big mall beside Amaeke town hall?" Emmanuel asked Ike.

"Yes, yes. The one that has plenty of good things inside. Emmanuel, did you see what I saw?" Ike queried.

"What did you see? Tell me…"

"Are you blind? Did you not see how people troop inside there, pick anything they want and then come over to pay those people at the table? Can't you see that it is the customers that display what they picked themselves while the cashiers do the calculation and get the customers to pay?" Ike continued.

"Ike, everyone knows that's the system there. What exactly are you driving at?"

"Emmanuel you are just not being smart this afternoon. Why? Can't you read the handwriting on the wall? Are you not seeing a golden opportunity? Look well or rather think well and see a business proposal right before you." Ike threw a punch line. Emmanuel smiled sheepishly exposing his gapped teeth.

"Are you thinking what I am thinking?" Emmanuel asked Ike.

"If what you are thinking is what I am thinking, then we are thinking the same thing." Both boys burst into laughter.

"Oh! Wait, Ike, do you not think we should engage the service of boys in our gang?" Emmanuel suggested.

"Haba! Emmanuel, for a task as meager as this? There is no need for that. I can singlehandedly run this business, just that I like doing things together with you. So please, are we good to visit Amaeke tomorrow?" Ike asked Emmanuel.

"Sure!" Emmanuel responded.

Unknown to Ike and Emmanuel, there were CCTV cameras at every strategic point in the shopping mall. This was such that, from the moment one entered the mall, to the time he left, every activity was being captured and recorded by the camera. Little did they know.

For information's sake, it was boldly written and pasted at the sliding entrance door for the view of everyone.

"CCTV cameras available. Do not take anything you are not willing or able to pay for!"

Either of these two things was the problem, it was either Ike and Emmanuel did not see the warning post or they didn't understand the meaning or function of CCTV. But whatever the case was, it was ignored by the duo.

The confidence level of Ike and his friend was boosted when they entered the mall and nobody neither stopped them nor gave them a different look, considering their age. They immediately went out of sight and started picking a few things putting them inside the basket they carried.

The security personnel in charge were surprised when they came out from the shopping section into the security post dumping everything they have picked at the doorway to the shopping section.

"Hey boys, you are expected to pick your basket to the cashier's post, that is where you make your payments and not leave them at the doorway where everyone passes." One of the security personnel cautioned.

"No sir. We don't want to buy again." Emmanuel replied to the surprise of the security men. How do you mean lads? You do not just pick items and claim you are no longer interested. Just like that? We do not allow that here!" Another security man added.

"Emm... Sir, we just noticed that my brother lost the money with which our mother sent us to buy these things. We want to go and look for it and then come back again." Just as Ike was rounding off, a staff from the management came and said a few things into the ear of one of the security personnel which signaled him to search both boys.

"May we search you, please."
"No!" The boys shouted on top of their voices, they began to tremble and shake as they least expected they would be suspected, let alone be searched.

They resisted the gentle approach of the security personnel until they applied force. They were both taken to the security room where they were stripped naked and to the amazement of the men, three gold wrist-watches fell off each boy's body. They were astonished. They did not believe that little boys of their age would come to a mall as big as the mall to steal three gold wrist-watches which are worth over three hundred thousand each of them. What would they use such money for? Perhaps they do not even know the worth of what they had stolen.

For Ike and Emmanuel, that was the worst day of their lives. The kind of punishment meted out on them was one they had never experienced in their lives. They were both hanged in the air with their hands tied to a rope which it's other end was perfectly knotted to the ceiling. And from where they were hung, each of them were given sixty heavy strokes of the cane after which they both passed out upon themselves. When they finally gained consciousness, they waited and cried. They continually swore never to engage in stealing again, but no one paid attention to them.

Mr. Paul, on second thought, decided to take up their case on a personal ground. He decided to get to the root of this crime and to know if they were sent by any external person.

Ike confessed after so many tortures from the security personnel that he masterminded the crime and that he compelled Emmanuel to join him.

"What do you need such stolen items or money for?" Mr. Paul asked.

"I use it to eat and pay my sister's school fees," Ike answered.

Mr. Paul and his security personnel were taken aback. Never had it been heard that a boy of fifteen years took up such responsibilities. Mr. Paul made further investigations and found out that the boy was telling the truth. He also found out that Emmanuel's parents were dead and that single-handedly sent him into the streets. Mr. Paul took some policemen to Abana and arrested John and Maria, after Ike had told them about the parental insecurity he and his sister, Vivian received from their parents.

John and Maria were kept under police custody for a period of two months during which Mr. Paul sent some counselors who advised them on the best way on parenting regularly.

Also, during this period, Mr. Paul took in Ike and Vivian, who had written her Common Entrance Examination, and waited for their parent's release.

Ike turned a new leaf, he went back to most people he had stolen from and asked for their forgiveness including Mrs. Vanessa.

Mr. Paul enrolled him back into primary five and he improved academically.

The experiences John and Maria met within the prison were not friendly at all. They were compelled to sign an undertaking with the police force to turn into better parents and to work together to achieve a better family and take care of their children.

"By this agreement, you are to become better parents and your children are never to be seen anywhere in the streets or fend for themselves. Any action contrary to this agreement is punishable by the law," said the policeman who shook hands with John and his wife.

John and Maria went over to the counter, picked up their belongings, and made their way home. They had resolved to make amends and build a better home.

MORAL LESSON

1.   Offenders should be reprimanded or punished.

2. Some matters need to be investigated thoroughly.

3. CCTV cameras are good for monitoring crimes in every big organization, shops and the society.

4. Parents need to know more about parenting if they want to build a Godly home.

5. People should come to the aid of those that needs to be helped.

QUESTIONS

1. What did an old aged adage say?

____

____

2. Which town was bigger than Ababa?

____

____

3. Where did Ike and Emmanuel go stealing?

____

____

4. What happened to them there?

____

5. What agreement or undertaking did John and Maria sign at the police station?

____

____

www.ingramcontent.com/pod-product-compliance
Lightning Source LLC
Chambersburg PA
CBHW072122150726

47999CB00005B/2084